FERRETS

*Taking their work & welfare
into the 21st Century*

by Simon Whitehead

published by Pakefield Ferrets

Published by:

Pakefield Ferrets
Pakefield
Lowestoft
Suffolk

www.pakefieldferrets.co.uk

ISBN Number 0-9539337-0-9

Foreword

As the countryside has changed over the years so has the purpose of keeping ferrets. Many are no longer used for pest control purposes but kept as pets. This does not always mean that the ferret keepers of the present time are given as much guidance and assistance as they once might have been as the skills of ferreting were often passed on from father to son and pest controller to his apprentice out in the fields. This also means that the bond that unites man to his *working* companion has been weakened.

This is an essential handbook for today's ferret keepers, written by someone who has worked with ferrets all his life and shares a deep respect for them. In a friendly and down-to-earth-manner, it covers all aspects of ferret husbandry along with the full range of advice for the ferreter. Simon has not only spent many years working with ferrets but has many, many hours of experience over past years of talking to people at events throughout East Anglia and giving others the benefit of his experience. Therefore he has been able to give answers to all the most essential questions, using his first hand knowledge of both ferrets and the people that ask the questions.

Richard Burge
Chief Executive
Countryside Alliance

Acknowledgements

I am very grateful to the following for their generous help during the writing of this book:-

My parents for putting up with me at all hours before shows; my brother David, for the use of all his knowledge on the computer, not only in this book but for many hours during the years helping me get my show set-ups right.

Paul, fellow ferreter, for all of his flexibility and commitment over the seasons; Darren and Tiggy, for the use of so much ferreting ground; Rodent Service E.A. Ltd., my employers, for their help in insuring that I can fulfil all my show commitments.

I am particularly grateful to all at the Countryside Alliance, both at a local level and headquarters in London for their help, support and technical back-up and to the vast majority of the public I have encountered at country and game fairs, as it is their lack of understanding of the ferret that has spurred me on to write this book.

But most of all to the person who keeps me going and has to put up with all my moods during the long year, both working and attending shows and fairs, Jules. Without her support and encouragement none of this would have made it past the initial idea.

Simon Whitehead

Contents

Chapter 1

Introduction

Never has an animal been so misunderstood, so frowned upon by the misinformed. Ask anyone for a description of a ferret and you would think they were describing some sort of monster, "A vicious, smelly creature that granddad used to keep hidden away at the bottom of the garden."

I have been attending county shows and game fairs over the years with my ferrets and there is one outstanding fact that has not only rooted firmly in my memory, but has spurred me on to write this book. Thousands of people experience my business of ferrets each year and whatever background they come from they are united by one major fact, their lack of knowledge of the ferret.

Go past the basic, and I mean basic, requirements and the majority struggle. I am sorry to have to say this but I'm afraid it's true. Whatever the ferret is to be used for, please remember that the needs of all ferrets are exactly the same, whether they are to be worked or kept as pets, or both. With this book I aim to put the final nail in the coffin of the ferret's old image and take the work and welfare of the ferret into the new millennium.

To many the word ferret sparks fear, fear of a smelly, spiteful animal that bites. Is this true or is it just plain ignorance rearing its ugly little head again? This image of the ferret started many moons ago when the ferret was domesticated to do a specific job. Yes, helping us catch food for the table.

Many people in today's society don't want to hear this but by nature we are hunters who through the ages have relied on hunting for our survival. If not, we wouldn't be here today which is a point we must all bear in mind.

The ferreter of old was an anonymous character who was seen but not heard. For some reason he struggled with this animal, the ferret. Here we have a carnivore, expertly adapted to hunting, a natural athlete. So what does the ferreter do? He keeps it in a small hutch and feeds it bread and milk! As I said earlier, mankind has a habit of fearing things it doesn't understand but, thankfully, some did try to understand and this is where the breakthrough came. Instead of being treated like a garden tool - only brought out when needed, kept locked away at the bottom of the garden and replaced when broken - today's ferret is not just a working animal but a wonderful creature, full of surprises, with endless enthusiasm that many would be proud of. I know some of you reading this disagree but it's true. How times have changed!

Not only will it work its heart out as nature intended but it offers many people a pet that is more adaptable than any rabbit or guinea pig, offering countless hours of fun to its owners, young and old alike. Like all animals they have needs, they need to be managed sensibly and properly. Hopefully after this book is read they will be! The days of neglect through ignorance are over. Education is, I believe, the way forward, not only for the ferret's sake, but without overloading the brain with deep science. I will leave that to others.

So you want a ferret but want to know more?
Before acquiring a ferret there are some basic requirements you will need to know. Firstly, never, ever, buy an animal on the spur of the moment. Whilst attending the Alliance stands at shows I see how people react to my ferrets. The vast majority automatically want one which is why I don't agree with people selling ferrets at shows. Who knows what fate has in store for

the poor ferret? You must first find out the facts, both for and against.

What do you keep it in, what do you feed it, how do you care for it, and what demands does it make? These are all subjects I hope to deal in the forthcoming chapters, so continue ferreting through this book and hopefully your questions will be answered. Firstly, remember that ferrets can live up to, and beyond, eight years of age and as their welfare improves their life span extends. There is no magical recipe to keeping ferrets. No, I tell a lie, there is, and here it is: suitable accommodation; a healthy diet; plenty of handling/socialization; and last but not least, good breeding stock from which your kits will come. This recipe will ensure that not only do you have a contented ferret but that it will live to a ripe old age with you. Nothing could be simpler so why do so many people struggle?

'Treat them mean, keep them keen.' This was unfortunately the norm in the old days and helped to create the image that I, along with the rest of the nation of ferret keepers, want to eradicate. So I hope that not only the newcomer will read and keep this for reference in times of need but also the more experienced keeper who wishes to know a little bit more about the animal that he or she has kept for years.

To get the best from your ferret you need to understand not only the history of the ferret but, more importantly, why it was domesticated in the first place to produce this fascinating creature we have today. The history of the ferret is vast, too vast for my pen. I am concerned about the future of the ferret so I will delve into the past when I really need to, when it is truly relevant. I'll leave the historian's hat to writers who are best suited to it.

The ferret, like all animals that have been domesticated, has been so for a reason, either to be used for working purposes or for enjoyment as a pet. A domesticated animal needs to serve a purpose but more importantly it needs a purpose to serve. In the ferret's case this purpose is hunting.

So why the ferret?

If you take a look at the relatives of the ferret they all share the same characteristics. The family includes such creatures as the otter, mink, polecat (of course), stoat and weasel, and the appearance of all its members is basically the same. The body has been adapted to suit the lifestyle and survival of the animal. The ferret is no different. They are all built for survival, some primarily in water, some in trees, some underground or in deep undergrowth and in some cases all these have been adopted, as in the case of the mink - possibly the perfect all round hunting machine.

The polecat was seen as the perfect animal to domesticate for the purpose of catching rabbits. The rabbit wasn't introduced to our shores until Norman times, presumably for food, and fur for clothing their troops. The natives had probably heard of how overseas the polecat was tamed to help catch this source of food in the hedgerows and woodlands of Europe. There is some mystery as to which polecat the ferret is descended from, the Steppe or the European. I hope the latter but that is just my opinion. They are so closely related they can crossbreed to each other just the same as the ferret can to the polecat.

Domestication was most probably reached by the method previously practised on animals by man. First they would have captured young kits from the polecats and tried to hand tame them. I say 'try' because remember that these are wild animals at this stage and therefore share their characteristics. After taming they would then breed from a captive male and female and handle the young until they had no fear of humans and didn't see them as a threat to their food. Once this was achieved, and generations of these animals had passed, a level of domestication was maintained. The social pecking order was then born as they accepted that man is at the top of the food chain and relied on him for their food.

An animal that trusts its owner, like all animals but especially dogs, needs to be trained, not only for the animals' benefit but for their acceptance into our way of life. A disruptive or destructive dog is a liability - the same applies to the ferret.

As I said earlier, the ferret over the years has evolved around the human world, his senses being fine tuned to those that are most beneficial to his survival, with those that are not used being toned down. As the ferret spends most of its time underground eyesight is not a top priority and is generally poor. The other senses make up for this as the senses of smell and hearing are acute.

To protect this bundle of senses we have a good fur coat, coarse outer hair with a softer protective coat beneath it. The part of the ferret that most people remember is its mouth, a mouth full of sharp canine teeth. This is a point I emphasise to the public to prevent them from sticking their fingers into the ferret run.

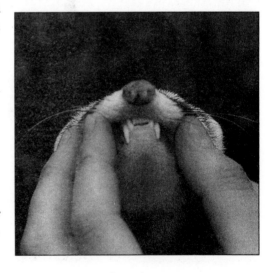

This picture shows the legendary canine teeth.

When you take a closer look at the ferret you will notice the elongated body, lean and muscular, with short legs. The feet have pads under the soles and sharp claws. These claws are vital to the everyday activities of the ferret. If your run or hutch has a concrete or hardwood floor this will be sufficient when the animal scrapes to keep the claws down. The trend amongst some ferret owners is to clip these claws short, very short, for show purposes which only inhibits the animals as it is a 'three dimensional' animal and needs claws for activities such as climbing and digging.

So there we have it, a brief insight into the bundle of fur you have decided to keep. But let us take a closer look at the differences between the sexes. The **jill** (female) and **hob** (male) dif-

fer considerably, especially in the springtime which is the mating season. The jill is smaller than the hob, her head more streamlined as opposed to the pug head of the male, which is broader and more compact. The body of the hob is usually about a third larger than that of the jill. This is called sexual dimorphism.

The Hob and the Jill.

Glossary of ferret terms

Jill   Female ferret

Hob   Male ferret (sometimes called a buck or jack)

Kit   Ferret aged less than 16 weeks

Hoblet   A ferret that has had a vasectomy

Hobble   A ferret that has been castrated

Business   The collective name for a group of ferrets.

The origins of all ferret colours, the polecat ferret and the albino.

Chapter 2

Housing

One of the biggest changes in the ferret revolution has been their housing. What we must not forget is that whatever housing we choose for our ferret this is the ferret's world - when not out in our company this is all the ferret sees and breathes so the least we can do is give them a respectful house. After all, how would you like to live in the equivalent of some of the hutches ferrets have been forced to live in? Because of the lack of basic knowledge of many ferret keepers the ferret was, and in some cases still is, kept in ill-designed and cramped hutches.

Today, I believe, we have a new breed of ferret keeper, a person who wants to learn how to get the best from the ferret - to put the needs of the ferret first. There are two categories; the working ferret and the pet ferret, although some are both. One thing unites both categories and this is their welfare.

When deciding what housing will be best suited to your needs there are a couple of questions that will have to be answered first. In the back of your mind you will already know how many ferrets you are going to keep, perhaps with the scope for more. What is important when choosing your housing is to consider:

1. The space required for the housing

2. The cost

3. The design best suited not only to the ferret but also to you (after all it is you who will be cleaning it)

Remember, the world of your ferret revolves around its housing so make sure you take the time to make it the right one. After all, how would you like to be cramped up all day and then be expected to be in peak physical and mental condition to perform any task asked of you?

There are many different types of housing starting with hutches and going through to ferret courts, with every conceivable modification in between.

The three main factors to be considered with the housing are:

1. Shelter from the elements - in all seasons.

2. Adequately draught-proof sleeping quarters

3. Security - not only to prevent the escape of the ferret but to stop the rogue figure from taking the ferret out of its home.

The first option we will look at is the ferret hutch, or cub, as it is traditionally known. The most common mistake made by the newcomer is to think that a rabbit hutch will be sufficient. This couldn't be further from the truth. Firstly, ferrets are 'three dimensional' animals, and therefore need room to satisfy not only their physical need to keep fit but their mental requirements as well. Play is enormously important to the development of the ferret as ferrets learn their hunting techniques through play, fighting and exploring pipes, etc. Not many rabbit hutches can give the ferret enough room to carry out these functions due to the fact that they were designed for rabbits, not ferrets.

The hutch must be large enough to fulfil these needs. The hutch can be as large as you wish but the minimum size should ideally be 4 ft. x 1 ft. 6 ins x 1 ft. 6 ins. (125 cm. x 45cm x 45 cm.)

The number of designs for your hutch are endless but your basic requirements will be roughly the same. The hutch needs to be able to withstand the unpredictable climate in which we live, designed to make cleaning easy but most importantly be secure enough to stop the ferret from escaping. The ferret is renowned for its ability to escape, a Houdini of the animal world.

Times have changed since I first started to keep ferrets, designs have altered, materials have changed, and even the preservatives used to weather-proof the wood are different, and I have seen how much of an improvement this has made to the well-being of the ferret.

The material from which you make your hutch has to be practical, manageable and workable. Wood is the most commonly used and probably the most cost-effective option. Plastics are sometimes used but these tend to be expensive. Plywood or hardboard is ideal but I would not recommend using chipboard like some I have seen recently. Not only will it soak up any liquid (such as preservative or urine) like ink on blotting paper, but it will then degenerate and provide routes for escape.

The design should be such that cleaning is made easier so you don't want a lot of gaps or obstructions, especially in the latrine corner. The hutch should preferably be screwed together to strengthen the structure.

It is up to you what design you decide on but the main thing is that the hutch is split into two separate compartments; the sleeping compartment and a run. The sleeping compartment must be solid, draught proof and have an entrance hole 2-3 ins. (5-7 cm.) round. This is to ensure that the sleeping quarters are dry, windproof and dark. In the summer it will enable the quarters to be cool, with less bedding than in the winter when the bedding is doubled for extra warmth.

The run of your hutch should have a wire front to the door section which will let light and fresh air circulate freely, as well as provide a place for the water bottle to be hung. The floor needs to be solid and secure with no ill fitting joints. On top of the hutch the roof needs to overhang at an angle to let rain safely drain away.

An option for those who want a bigger hutch but haven't got the ground space is to have a wire-run fixed securely to the underneath of the standing hutch which will instantly double the space that the ferret has access to but the standing space is the same.

A ferret hutch or cub

When it comes to weatherproofing your hutch, again there are several important points to take into consideration. The materials with which you can preserve your hutch have changed for the better. You must use non-toxic preservatives but these are commonly found in shops or stores. Creosote is poisonous to the ferret and under no circumstances should it be used. In days gone by paint was used which is all right on the outside but if used on the inside, although it looks nice and clean, sweats and creates condensation thus causing dampness inside the hutch, especially the sleeping quarters.

As you see in the photographs, the roof should be at an angle, slightly overhanging at the front. The hinges and brackets used should be strong enough for the task. Security should never be overlooked. Not only might a rogue want your well managed ferrets but also the opportunist thief might open the hutch out of curiosity. Padlocks are invaluable as they will deter many but nothing short of Fort Knox will keep your ferret 100% safe.

The position of your hutch is just as important as the design and building. The best-made hutch in the world will succumb to the elements if positioned incorrectly. Make sure it is positioned in an area out of direct wind and rain. As you are responsible for the management of the hutch make the height at which it stands comfortable to yourself and at a convenient height for you to carry out the cleaning.

One final thought on the position of your hutch; the seasons of the year change dramatically, there will be snow, ice and rain. Not only must the hutch be in an appropriate position, it must also be easy to walk to because the last thing you want to do is to destroy your best lawn by continually walking up and down in wet weather.

As an improvement to the hutch some people fill the gap below with a wire cage/run, securely fastened, as this adds extra space for the benefit of the ferret. If this is done the floor must be either concrete or patio slabs.

The second choice, and the one which I prefer, is the ferret court. The court system was the one preferred by the warreners of old as they could keep all their animals in one place. Not only did this make the management easier but it also gave the ferrets more room in which to exercise.

The court is a simple structure, the floor made of concrete or patio slabs. Some have used the more natural approach and used grass but this is impossible to keep clean, and cuts up when wet, therefore giving the ferret health problems because of constantly wet feet.

Those who have seen me at shows will know that I have a miniature court for my display team. This consists of a six feet square, four feet high court with a wire floor, which I cover with straw but this is just for convenience because the grounds on which shows are held are not always bowling greens.

Starting with the floor, this should be concrete - either in block flooring or slabs. If slabs are used, do remember to fill the gaps between them with cement. This will prevent any food or droppings being missed when cleaning. Concrete is not only easy to clean and disinfect but enables the ferret claws to be worn down naturally to a manageable level. On top of the floor we have the sides and roof of the court. Many materials can be used but the normal one is wood. The ideal size for this court would be 6 ft. x 6 ft. with a height of 6 ft. (2m. by 2m. with a height of 2m.) The height is important as, again, it is you who have to clean it out and working in uncomfortable conditions can lead to bad backs.

In many magazines and pet shops there are aviary panels for sale. These measure 2m. by 1m. and are ideal as you can construct to whatever size you wish and know it will be well built. The best way of fastening is with bolts and then if you need to move the court you simply unbolt it.

One aspect of the court which many people overlook is the roof. Ferrets are three-dimensional in their activities and although they are not as agile as the marten or mink they still love to climb, even to a height of two metres. A roof made of mesh is advisable unless you can ensure that there are no gaps for the occupant to find and escape through.

*A ferret
court*

Now that we have a court situated on concrete we will need something for the ferrets to sleep/rest in. As the ferret should have dry, windproof and secure sleeping quarters there are a number of options for the occupants. You could join the court to a small shed (like mine), or place small nest boxes inside the court, or place them on the outside for easier cleaning and checks. There should be enough boxes for the ferrets to give them not only space but escape routes if games get a bit rough.

The most practical design for a nest box is as shown on the next page. As you can see it is a manageable size with an entrance/exit hole and removable lid.

As with the hutch, the positioning is vital. I live on the cliffs in East Anglia and in the winter it gets very cold and windy. Taking this into account is why I fitted a small shed to my court

Nest box filled with shredded material.

as this enables the ferrets to have an indoor court as well.

Whatever design fits the bill for you and your ferrets, you will need bedding materials for the ferrets. On the floor of the run of your hutch/inside court you will need a covering of material to soak up the liquids that will be deposited. I would recommend using wood shavings as opposed to sawdust. Sawdust is very fine and will find its way into the ferrets' eyes and nasal passages, again creating a health risk. Wood shavings are much bigger so the risk is minimal. In the nest boxes you will need bedding. Straw or hay is most practical and is readily available anywhere. Lately in the shops I have seen shredded paper which is fine if it is not coloured. Coloured paper has a lacquer with arsenic residue in it and as arsenic is a poison I wouldn't have thought it would do your ferret any good.

Inside the hutch or court the ferret will need to have food and water. The water can be supplied via gravity-fed drinkers firmly fixed to the mesh of the walls. Water and ferrets make a fascinating match. As ferrets love to explore under objects the use of a water bowl would be one of comical consequences. Drinkers should be checked daily to ensure a fresh and free running supply of water. If you were housing a number of ferrets in a court perhaps you would be better off with a poultry drinker.

All water containers should be regularly cleaned to prevent a build up of algae, especially transparent drinkers during summer months.

The ferret's food should be in a broad based earthenware feeding bowl which is preferable to a plastic one as ferrets have a fascination with exploring. Everything has to be investigated, even underneath. and food bowls are often turned over within minutes of being put in.

As surely as night follows day, the ferrets' food is followed by the waste products - droppings. Cleaning is one of the most important tasks the ferret owner has to carry out. Although the ferret has an image of being a dirty, smelly animal nothing could be further from the truth. Ferrets are clean animals, not only spending large amounts of time grooming but they use the same toilet area time and time again, usually a corner furthest away from the nest area, which makes the cleaning easier.

But what to use? Listed below are some of the essential utensils needed to clean your hutch/court.

1.   Dustpan and brush

2.   Watering can

3.   Scraper

4.   Bottle of clean fresh drinking water

5.   Fresh shavings

6.   Fresh bedding

7.   Large bin liner

8.   Disinfectant

These tools should ensure that the ferret always has a clean and fresh home to live in. Because the ferret always uses the same toilet area, each morning/night just remove the droppings and sprinkle some fresh shavings. Check the water and replace if fully used.

At least once a week the premises should undergo a thorough cleansing and disinfecting. When using disinfectant make sure that it is ferret friendly. An easy way of testing this is if it turns water milky white, it isn't safe. (The substance to avoid is *phenol*.) Whatever cleaning substance you use stick to the instructions on the bottle and if the ferrets show any signs of discomfort, change it immediately.

Chapter 3

Food for thought

One of the biggest improvements in the welfare of ferrets nowadays is their diet. Never in the black hole of ferret history has so much thought and consideration gone into the diets of our animals. This is so the ferret of the future can be a healthier and happier ferret.

In all the sporting and ferret magazines, what and when to feed the ferret is a constant topic, with many of the so-called experts expressing such a variety of views that must seem frightening to the beginner or, come to think of it, to most ferreters. This is why it is important that we look at the different foods, their advantages and disadvantages. After all it has been said that we are what we eat so why feed an inappropriate diet? This not only affects the immune system and the general day to day well-being of the ferret but shortens the life-span of your animal as well, considerations that you must make before deciding which food/foods are best suited for your situation.

The balance must be right as in all aspects of ferret keeping. That is what this book is all about; building a wall brick by brick to keep the ignorance out of ferret keeping and ferreting. Before, in the days when men were men and ferrets were frightening, the person who wanted to keep a ferret only had a handful of people to ask for advice about its welfare. Sadly, these were the type of people who gave, and in some places still give, ferrets a bad name.

There were only a few books about and these just contained the same limited information, until the ferret revolution started. Books appeared on shelves containing logical and practical information on ferrets, acquired through experience and looking at how the ferret was being kept and worked, by realizing that this way was wrong and seeking to improve it - with great success. Year by year a new book would appear, building on the great start Fred J. Taylor had given to all of us. Don't be fooled though - this book was hailed by many as the ferret bible at the time but just like the Holy Bible you have to read it and follow by example and many of us don't. Don't get me wrong, I'm not a religious person - only where my ferrets are concerned.

This is where I feel that the ferret's feeding problems started. I'm not knocking the generations before me who kept ferrets because they really didn't know any different, with the blind leading the blind. The problem nowadays is that nobody likes either to change or to admit they were wrong.

Today we look at welfare through a different pair of glasses, reactalights I think they are called. These are more focused than before and instead of being dazzled by new information we can look straight into it and make up our own minds, looking and learning. This is one area that we have not only the few ferreters who blessed the pages of many sporting papers to thank but the pet fraternity. I know this won't go down too well in some places, but be fair, credit where credit's due.

Year by year pet owners looked after their ferrets, not working them but just enjoying their companionship, wondering how to improve their lifestyle. Being carnivorous, meat was the natural food for the ferret but if you don't work them and so don't have a constant source of meat, what then? They weren't satisfied with the concoctions they were told about which just weren't good enough for them.

Cats and dogs proved to be the turning point I think. Natural carnivores just like the ferret, they were being fed a mixed diet of meat based biscuits. Perhaps this was the future?

The main ingredient of a long and happy life for any animal is a balanced diet. The right mixture of vitamins, proteins, minerals, etc. This not only prolongs the lifespan of the ferret but makes the job of replacing all the effects of birth and stud duties that much easier.

The general misconception about ferrets and their feeding habits has stuck firmly since time began. This is still present today. Many people whom I see at fairs still advocate the starving of ferrets, believing that this will make them work harder, the idea being that because the animal is hungry it will work its heart out. This idea led to countless lay-ups and suggestions that the ferret is no good. I don't know about you but I work terribly on an empty stomach. If I saw a tasty meal would I ignore it? Of course not! So why expect the ferret to?

During the years after the initial myxy outbreak the ferret began its transformation from a predominantly working animal to a pet and pet/working animal. For the first time the ferret was being observed closely by pet owners who had time to as the demand for rabbits became less and less. Not many people will agree with me but I think we owe a huge debt to these early pet ferret owners with regards to the dietary needs of the ferret. Without them who knows at what stage we would be now?

Ferret keepers of old had little understanding of the needs of the ferret. Cost and availability, these were at the top of their list when it came to feeding the ferret and had a bigger bearing on the diet than anybody would care to admit. I suppose we are spoilt today because of all the time spent studying the old ways but they didn't have this benefit so they started with a diet of bread and milk. There couldn't be a meal further from ferrets' requirements, could there? This was to be the basis of the legendary ferret myth.

An unsuitable diet consisting of bread and milk resulted in an amazing increase in the smell of both animal and droppings, these representing the equivalent of diarrhoea. The ferret then began to get its smelly image. Because of the mixture of neglect in its handling and feeding, the hungry ferret was a bit more aggressive than a normal ferret of today's standards. This was their cry for help.

Then more and more keepers looked at its wild cousin for guidance and many things were discovered that changed how people fed their ferrets. The polecat, being a carnivore, fed on a rich and varied diet, from amphibians up to large mammals such as rabbits. Meat had to be the main basis of food they thought, many feeding the complete rabbit to the ferret. This was great as they contain everything from bones to fur for roughage but their cleaning regime let them down, and more often than not the carcass was left in the small hutch for a week or so, even in summer time. It wasn't a pretty sight, I can tell you. But everyone has to start somewhere.

Let's take a closer look at the foods available and how they affect the ferret. The health of a ferret and its diet can be judged by the state of its droppings (*faeces*). A ferret fed on a suitable diet should have dark, firm droppings with little odour. On the other hand a ferret fed on an unsuitable diet has the opposite; sloppy, light and very smelly - ugh! The diet also has an effect on the life span because fed a balanced healthy diet they will, or should, live a longer and happier life.

Way back in time when I were a lad, all the ferreters I knew fed milk slops. Even though I knew it was wrong, I knew the ferret was a carnivore, what could I do? I was a newcomer to the big, bad world of ferrets as it was then. But I was lucky, I learned all about these creatures from someone who had the best of both worlds: terrific working partners and excellent pets when not working, I saw both sides of the coin. Through the years I have seen many reflections of myself when I started who, dare I say it, are the next generation of ferreters who will make a difference.

But why feed a ferret an unsuitable food? Well, nowadays there are no excuses, unlike in years gone by. Just take a look around the country fairs of today, ferrets everywhere, but only recently has this been the case. The ferreter of the past had no one to ask, no one to look to for good advice, only the shady characters of country folklore. Even these people were reluctant to give away information that might have been useful, a far cry from the pool of knowledge we all have at our disposal today.

It is logical to say that the bigger the ferret the more food it will consume, but is it true? Ferrets' feeding is governed by their metabolism. A high one means the food is easily burnt off, a low one and it would be easy for the ferret to become fat and lazy. The ferret is less active in the summer and if the same amount of food is consumed as in the winter they are likely to get overweight. In the winter the body converts food into heat/energy so more is needed. The same is true for stud ferrets and expectant mothers, who need to store fats for the coming birth or replace what has been lost by the stresses and traumas of birth.

In the court system ferrets that are kept together will establish a pecking order for food so a careful watch must be kept to ensure that all are getting their fair share. Many believe in fasting the ferret for a day to recreate the past but I feel that as I wouldn't like to be starved for one day of the week I won't practise it on my animals. My ferret court has always a bowl full of food in it!

On the food front the ferret has been fed a number of diets, based on folklore, availability or what has been recommended.

The list below is of the more common meals that are being fed to ferrets, without touching on the ridiculous.

Bread and milk slops
This was the first food for the unfortunate ferret. Not only was it totally devoid of any nutrients but it gave the ferret scours (diarrhoea). This not only weakened the animal through malnutrition but shortened the average lifespan and is not to be recommended as a main source of food, but altered slightly can provide a treat for your ferret. Add an egg to the bread and milk, cook and leave to cool. Ferrets love it.

Whole or part carcass diet
The feeding of the whole carcass to ferrets has been carried out for years. This is the ideal meal for a carnivore such as the ferret but the problems associated with it spurred on the invention of the complete range of foods.

In an ideal world we could feed the ferret and it would eat up all its food, no problem. In the real world the ferret eats a little at a time and stores the rest, thus creating hygiene problems with flies and disease. Husbandry needed to be of a very high standard to combat this threat but more often than not it wasn't. The ferret then began to smell and the rest is history, as they say. The same can be said of most meat. Pet mince is too fatty, dog meat has no nutrients and the ferret becomes tired and lethargic on such diets.

Day-old chicks
This is one of the more recent food fashions to hit our shores. Popular with many for two reasons, firstly, they think because you are feeding a whole carcass the ferret is getting the right balance needed in a stable diet and secondly, they are cheap. For as little as two pence each they sound ideal. However, the down on these birds is very fine and builds up in the digestive tract of the ferret, causing infection. The bird itself, having just surfaced

from the egg, is low on calcium, protein and fat which causes low bone growth in young ferrets but this food can be fed as a treat to adult ferrets occasionally.

Dog and cat foods

These are widespread and ferrets will eat them but care must be taken. The majority of dog foods are deficient in the vitamin and mineral needs of ferrets so a substitute would have to be added to fulfil these needs. Cat food is slightly more acceptable because of its higher protein count but if regularly fed it must be in conjunction with a bonemeal powder (e37). This will ensure that the right amount of calcium is consumed to help the animals' bones and teeth.

All fresh meat diets must be either fresh or thoroughly thawed to avoid poisoning the ferrets.

Complete foods

On the market today there are several ferret foods. Although some are expensive, they offer the ferret owner a way of not only reducing the smell of ferret droppings by means of an added deodorizer in the food but eliminate the threat of flies because being a biscuit it can be fed *ad hoc* as it doesn't go off. This can be fed from weaning right throughout the life of the ferret. It can also be fed in conjunction with a little rabbit meat as is favoured by some.

Summary

There are many foods on the market so you can feed whatever suits you best but the ferret is your responsibility so cheap isn't always best. Consider the food carefully - it is the ferret that counts.

Water

This is the most important substance of all, without it nothing can survive. Water takes on an even more important role if your ferret is being fed a dry food diet. The water can be delivered three ways, two practically and one that courts disaster:-

1. The gravity-fed drinking bottle.

These come in a variety of sizes from small to large (usually made for rabbits).

2. The poultry drinker.

Available almost anywhere these are mostly used in courts where they are many ferrets housed together and the amount of water needed is substantial. This is more practical than having a lot of drinking bottles around the court.

3. The drinking bowl.

This was one of the earliest methods but taking into account the ferrets' nature kept being overturned.

WARNING

Because water is essential, regular checks should be carried out to ensure that it is clean and free flowing. More care must be taken in the winter as frost can damage drinking bottles. All drinking bottles must be cleaned out regularly to prevent a build up of algae which will give the ferret upset stomachs if allowed to build up. To remove algae from bottles, fill the bottle a quarter full with sand, add a little water and shake like mad. Rinse out all the contents and the bottle should be clean.

Always check, maintain and fill bottles regularly.

Caution

There are many foods which are potentially lethal to ferrets including sugar or sugar saturated foods, alcohol, human chocolate and nuts. Many people like to give their ferrets treats now and then but the ferret is a small animal so any treats must be fed in moderation. Please be careful and give healthy treats, which will benefit the animal and not endanger its health.

Chapter 4

Your Ferret

The dilemma of purchasing a ferret, or any animal come to think of it, is one of the most underestimated aspects of ferret keeping. I would like to promise that all ferreters have the same standards but I'm afraid I can't, which is the whole point of this book being written to spell out the pitfalls to avoid, not just for your sake but for the benefit of the ferret.

The ferret's average lifespan is eight years which is an awfully long time if the ferret is allowed to become an unsuitable companion. That is why it's vital the right choice is made in the first place. Many a hopeful ferret keeper has been either put off or had their enthusiasm dampened by the wrong choice. What is the hurry? There are ferrets everywhere looking for stable, considerate homes, be they workers, pets or both. The one thing I cannot promise in this book is that you will not make a mistake. After all, the chances of me being there when you purchase the ferret are slim!

Although the best age to get a ferret is when it is young some people prefer adult animals and rescue and welfare societies are the perfect place to start. Although some are better than others they all share the pressure of countless careless owners who abandon their animals through neglect or lack of time. If only this book had been available earlier for these people.

The most popular and, I believe, best time to acquire a ferret is when it is ready to leave the mother - about eight weeks old. Kits as they are known, are available in the summer, due to the ferrets' breeding season (see chapter on Welfare). There are various ways of contacting people with ferrets for sale. First, try the local rescue centres, read the adverts in the local papers or, better still, search the country shows.

Nowadays at shows the ferret exhibitors on Countryside Alliance or similar stands will be willing to help you. Never buy a ferret as a result of a spur of the moment decision.

Like all animals the ferret's attributes are carried in its genes. It is therefore important to take care when choosing stock. Don't be bullied or panicked into buying the first ferret you see. There are plenty more ferrets out there. Ask to see the parent animals, see them handled and where they live, what food they are fed, examine their stools. It is highly likely that some of the traits in the mother are going to be passed down to her young. If you are happy with the parents and they are what you want, the next question is which colour and sex you require/prefer.

Let me put a myth to bed. The only difference between the vast range of colours is the colour of their hair. It makes no difference to the character, working ability or temperament and only you will know which colour you prefer.

Ferrets have a wide range of colours, ranging from the albino with pink eyes through to the dark polecat colouring. Some people think that there are two types of ferret, the albino and the polecat but, as I said, the only difference is the colour of their hair. Personally I prefer the polecat marked ferret as I think it has more character appeal because of the markings but this is just my personal opinion.

The next choice is what sex and how many? What problems will it bring if the wrong combination is chosen? For the novice, it is probably best keeping jills (females) together. It is best to keep more than one because they are sociable animals and enjoy the company of others. This is a far cry from their cousin, the polecat, which lives in solitude.

The combinations that could be chosen are the following three:

1. Two jills

2. Two hobs

3. One hob and one jill

Two jills are probably the best combination, but remember that in spring they come into season and must be taken out (see chapter on Welfare). You could overcome this by having them neutered.

The two hobs would be fine until the spring when they come into season then they will get aggressive towards each other. To overcome this you could get both hobs castrated which would also reduce the smell of the ferret.

Keeping a natural pair together has the ultimate problem. When spring arrives, the hob will come into season before the jill and if they are not separated by the time the jill comes into season nature will take its course. Remember a litter can be up to and beyond twelve kits which take a lot of looking after, feeding and placing in new homes.

Be a responsible owner
So, you have got a suitable hutch, you know what food you need, and have got it ready inside the hutch. You've looked around and selected your kits and finally you've brought them home - what now?

Ferrets, especially young kits, have plenty of character. This will develop as they grow up and will have a big bearing on how they will perform both in the field and as pets. There is one thing that makes a ferret stand out from other pets - you can *never* handle, stroke, talk to or play with a ferret too much.

As they grow up several stages in their socialization must be taken. The first, and most important, step is when your new ferrets arrive. Leave them in their new surroundings for a while, perhaps over night, as this is a big wrench. Imagine that after eight weeks of living with a mother and nine brothers and sisters, having a party, being pulled out, put in a carrying box and placed in a big strange hutch. Yes, this is quite daunting so let the kits settle in before you start pulling them out to be played with.

There are several ways of getting the ferret used to the hands and I am going to share with you the method which has worked successfully for me over the years. Firstly, you must know how to hold a ferret. There are a number of misconceptions which keep cropping up. The majority of ferrets do not bite, as I said earlier. If the parents have been fed, handled and looked after well there is little danger of their youngsters becoming biters - it is uncommon for ferrets to be born biters.

The character of both you and your ferret will be tested in the coming months. The main thing to remember is that little ferrets will not only mentally and physically grow quickly, so will their teeth and naturally, like puppies, they will want to explore with them but with a cool, calm and collected attitude you can easily handle any obstacles that might appear.

The voice must be used as a tool. The ferret will get used to it and be excited at the prospect of you coming to take it out of its hutch into the big world outside the mesh front. Always talk to your ferret when handling it, be calm and pick it up in one swift action. Any animal has the capability of detecting the slightest hesitancy and tends to play on it. The ferret is no different.

A ferret that is both used to being handled and played with is a joy to own. The ferret thinks that every time you approach the hutch or pick it up is enjoyable and will gladly comply. There are two ways of picking up a ferret:-

1.   Pick up and hold the ferret as you would a cat. Talk to it, stroke it and then pick it up with your hand round the stomach, the ferret laying in the palm of your hand. This method is fine if you are familiar with the ferret, but what happens if you are uncertain of the reaction of a ferret?

2.   Pick up the ferret by putting your thumb and forefinger gently around the its neck. This will give the ferret the security it craves but, more importantly, the ferret cannot turn around and, God forbid, bite you. This hold is useful when dealing with rescues.

If a ferret becomes restless or aggressive try swinging and stroking the back and stomach. This calms ferrets to such an extent that I have sent them to sleep in my hands at shows. If a ferret is pregnant extra caution is a must. Help the ferret's weight by holding around the neck and support the rest with your hand. Practise these holds as much as you possibly can. Sometimes you come across a large hob that it would be a struggle to hold around the neck without strangling in which case you will have to support him by his chest and neck.

The next stage is to get the ferrets used to the hands in all different situations, not just when they are being picked up out of their hutch. Put the ferrets on the ground and proceed to tickle them and rub their stomachs in a playful manner. This simulates the rough play of the mother with her kits which forms a background to their hunting skills if in the wild.

As these kits have ever-growing teeth they want to explore everything with them. Just as with a puppy or kitten, you must discourage it by chastising the animal. The kit will attempt to nip you as it would its fellow kits, it is perfectly natural, but what you must do is get it out of the habit of nipping you and start to teach it the difference between you and a kit. How can we teach the ferret the difference and show it that hands are not on the menu, ever?

That is where the rough play comes in. Antagonize the ferret by this play, believe me it won't take much to make the kit nip, and when it strikes, so must you.

This is done by either pinching the nose or by flicking the nose with your finger.

To a small ferret kit this has the same impact as if we were hit over the head with a baseball bat. Don't get me wrong, it is not cruel and we are using the minimum of force. I don't know about you but I wouldn't need many hits to get the message across. Every time this exercise is carried out the kit should be rewarded afterwards when it behaves itself. Make a fuss of it, feed it a tidbit. Carry on with this game until the ferret grows tired of it and refuses to even look at your fingers.

The next step is to place a drop of milk on your finger and let the ferret lick it off. When the milk has disappeared the kit will examine your finger and probably nip it. In the same way as before, chastise it. Your finger is yours, you need it, it is not on the menu.

Continue these simple exercises each day adding a stern, "No," to the chastisement, which will reinforce to the ferret what is right and what is wrong.

The ferret kit's teeth are growing all the time, from birth up to about sixteen weeks. This is a point worth remembering when acquiring a ferret for the first time. It is a lot easier to imprint and teach a small kit of eight weeks than a nearly full grown sixteen week old ferret. For one thing the milk teeth of the young kit don't hurt whilst a fully grown set are a different story, but also the brain is at the same stage. Remember the saying, "You cannot teach an old dog new tricks."

Handle and play with your ferrets as much as possible to make being your friends and companions for the next six years or so that little bit more worthwhile.

Chapter 5

Ferret welfare

Health, happiness, prosperity and general well-being are what we all hope for in life and what we should provide for the animals we keep and work. Many books and articles have been written about ferret welfare but little on how the beginner, or otherwise, can carry out practical ferret welfare. Welfare is a subject that has completely changed, not only our general perception of the ferret but the way in which we keep these animals.

Because of the way we are, when the subject was raised it was scorned by many who knew very little about it, mainly the working fraternity. This is when the ferret revolution truly kicked in. More and more ferreters were keeping them as pets as well as working their animals by the time the dreaded myxy struck. There was no need for the large number of ferrets kept pre-myxy, but some owners just could not bear to get rid of the animals who had given them years of pleasure. Enter the beginning of the ferret as a pet.

Ferrets were kept as pets for the younger generation and handled to the point of boredom. They were housed in large hutches, which Dad was nagged to make and their diet was studied more radically.

"Dad, why is the ferret fed bread and milk when it is a carnivore?" was the norm. Only then did people start to look at the needs of the ferret. Don't get me wrong, there have always been isolated pockets of people who fed meat to their ferrets and cleaned up after them but these were rare.

As these children grew so the knowledge grew and more adults began keeping ferrets as pets. Better housing and more research into their diet was going on and the whole subject of welfare was gaining momentum. But were the old school listening? No!

I call them the 'old school' because today the ferreter has more of a database to go to for information about ferrets than his predecessors. This is often forgotten in the magazines we read week by week, articles about these so-called experts and their feeding regimes.

Both the pet and working ferret keepers have their faults. Perhaps the pet owners are taking the term 'pet' to the extreme. The show people who clip, poke and prod may be a little too much. Is it in the interest of the ferret to breed for mutated hair length, exaggerated colours and sizes? Well, they think it is and only time will tell.

Compare the two types of working ferreter:

1.   The old school ferreter keeps anything from a single ferret up to about fifty at any one time. Basic, very basic, husbandry, feeds a poor diet or a proper diet but doesn't clean often enough.

2.   The modern ferreter takes a pride in his ferrets and is not afraid to show people his love for them. Maintains good stock, husbandry, diet and general welfare. When working his attitude is 'the ferret comes first.'

Compare the two and reach your own conclusion. What do you want for your ferrets? Ferreter No. 2 has evolved as a result of seeing the condition of the pet ferret and learning from the mistakes of the old school who do still exist I can assure you; old keepers, warreners and so-called pest controllers, all people who really should know better.

One of the questions I am most frequently asked at fairs is, "Are they easy to keep?" It doesn't take a lot to keep a ferret happy. Keep them clean, dry and fed properly and provide plenty of socialization. An easy task, so why do so many struggle with it?

The latrine corner should be cleaned daily, the water bottle filled and plenty of food given. If feeding meat it is necessary to check for left overs to prevent them going off. This is one area where complete, dry food has revolutionized the way we feed our ferrets.

As a rule the ferret is a hardy little creature which we have underestimated in the past despite their enormous appetite to please. The Houdinis of the animal world, they can also be excellent actors. The ferret hides its health problems in much the same as its wild cousin. In the wild an animal that shows weakness when ill is a target which can be an annoying trait in a ferret as sometimes it can be critically ill before anything is shown to be wrong.

Later on in this chapter I will go through the more common ailments that affect the ferret but first I will tackle the most talked about ferret subject.

Jills, their breeding and seasons

We have all heard the tales of the old ferreter, "If I don't breed her she'll die." The same person then moans later that he is overrun with ferret kits. As time goes by, modern scientific methods mean that we can deal with all sorts of problems, food and now welfare. Because the ferret has become a popular pet vets are now seeing more of them, thus gaining a better understanding of them. One benefit of this has been the way we have of dealing with ferrets in season (*oestrus*).

As is the case with most animals, the season is governed by the expanding hours of daylight during the day (*photoperiodism*). The ferret, like the wild polecat, will come into season when the daylight is greater than darkness. In the case of the polecat this is so the kits have the best possible start to life. Not only is it warm but because of the time of year the mother will have a large supply of food to choose from because of all the other animals breeding and having the great outdoors to explore.

We have now established that if the female ferret (jill) is not taken out of season, she will remain in season throughout the summer months. To the novice this might sound a bit daunting but, believe me, it isn't. When the jill is coming into season her vulva will swell up to the size of a peanut (see picture).

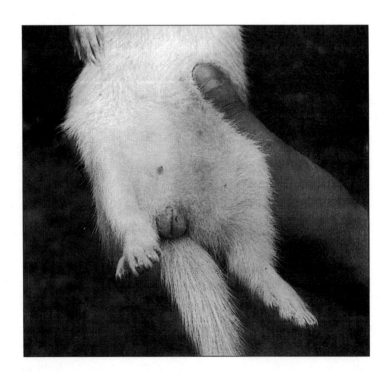

If the jill is not taken out of season by whatever method her body will react to the female sex hormone *oestregen* which is continually racing around her body. If not acted upon eventually this will cause a depression of all the three types of blood cells present which is potentially fatal in ferrets, if not in the same year the next one or even later. If she is not removed from this cycle the ferret may not fulfil her expected lifespan. On the other hand, I have known countless ferrets live to a ripe old age without being removed from season. There are always exceptions to the rule, aren't there?

With the jill's season forthcoming, several options appear to the owner :-

1. Do I want to breed ?

2. Am I ever going to breed ?

3. Do I take her to the vet for an injection?

4. Is there a hoblet available?

If you are sure, I mean 100% sure, that you are not going to breed from your ferret the most practical option is neutering. Jills will never need to be removed from season and the hobs won't fight, thus making housing hobs together easier. The accidental patter of tiny feet is avoided and the build up of aggression in the hobs is removed. Not only is the smell reduced but the ferrets can be kept in any order sexually.

If you don't want to neuter or you think that you may want to breed the jill an injection might be the answer. The jill jab is one of the more scientific ways of removing the jill from her season and most vets are happy to administer it but it is always advisable to check. For most owners the jill jab is the most convenient method available as it is safe, cost effective and leaves the door open for breeding at a later time.

If you have a number of jills you might want to select the natural method. A hoblet is a male that has undergone a vasectomy at the vet's, an operation which usually costs around £30-£40. This little fellow can then carry out the service of jill removal for the rest of his life therefore he will repay many times over. This method is fast becoming a more popular option. People like the natural method because many don't like to fill their ferrets with drugs if they can avoid it.

When taking your jill out of season with a hoblet, because it is totally natural to the animals, another natural thing sometimes happens, well, almost. Using a hoblet sometimes causes a phantom pregnancy *(pseudo* pregnancy). The jill will exhibit all the signs of the real thing, swollen teats, producing milk, nest-making, all the signs but with one real difference. At the end of the forty-two days she will think she has had a litter. Because I keep all my jills together, if one has a phantom she tends to think of the others as her babies which can be annoying during shows as she will tend to drag the others back to the nest box all the time, however large they are.

The jill will usually come back into season in the summer and mate with the hoblet again. The breeding season is then over as the hours of darkness outnumber those of daylight. The ferret will not come back into season that year.

At this point I feel I must issue a warning concerning hoblets. All animals can carry disease and the ferret is no different. Aleutian disease, flu and other diseases can be transmitted by the ferret. It is irresponsible of ferret owners if they do not resist the temptation to loan the ferret to all and sundry and do not check beforehand. There are tests available for Aleutian disease which give peace of mind. The cost is minimal but the advantages are priceless.

Because of the increased opportunities vets are getting to further their knowledge of ferrets the future should see better cared for jills and fewer unwanted kits in overworked rescue and welfare societies.

So you want to breed your ferret

As with dogs and racehorses we all want to further our own line of animals and the ferret is the same. Responsible ownership includes responsible attitudes towards breeding to prevent unleashing more unwanted kits into the world. You must be breeding for the right reasons.

If as described earlier, your jill is coming into season, you want to breed and you need new stock, the characteristics of the ferrets need to be looked at seriously. Whatever your reason for breeding the future of your ferret is at stake.

The stud ferret should be vetted thoroughly because a lot of your future ferret's characteristics are in the father, e.g. colour, size and workability. (If like many people you just want a pet then the latter will be of no importance).

Remember, you know the ins and outs of your jill but if you are using another person's hob you need to be 101% certain that it is what you want and not just the first available. If you want the best results put the best ingredients into the pot. Make a mental list of what you want and stick to it. Whatever the relations of the ferrets, whether it's line or cross breeding, the results will be the same. So look, make up your mind and go for it.

Many different colours are obtainable through different crosses. Too many in fact. I am not going to delve into the chasm of genetics over coloration, I'll leave that to the experts. The colour of your ferret is a matter of personal choice, whether it's a polecat or albino. Remember that all ferrets are the same underneath, it's only the colour of hair that is different.

The mating of ferrets is not a pretty sight. Thankfully, things are different in our world. The whole procedure is a violent, noisy one. The jill totally submits herself to the hob who in return drags her around by the neck until the mating is over. That's nature for you!

To have a successful mating the hob needs to be fertile. While this is normal you do sometimes find the odd sterile hob. Although annoying to your breeding plans it could save you the cost of a vasectomy operation.

After the rough and ready mating ritual the pregnancy will last between 42-44 days. The jill will use all her health and strength during the pregnancy so it is imperative that she gets a top quality diet.

As I tend to keep all my ferrets in a court I leave the pregnant jill inside this until fourteen days before the birthing date when she is placed in a separate hutch. This not only gives her time to get accustomed to the hutch but also to being alone, which to some comes as a greater shock than actually giving birth.

The birth can produce a litter of anything up to, and beyond, twelve but the average is between six and ten. The proud new mother will keep her little ones away from prying eyes for a while so unless you have a particularly good bond with your ferret I would advise you to give her a little time to adjust to the kits. If you are worried and really need to see them, keep your visit to a minimum to avoid upsetting the mother. You will have many anxieties if it is your first time but let me put your mind at rest. Ferrets have been giving birth for a long time, they're perfectly adapted to the job.

From birth you will hear their high pitched squeals while they are feeding on mother's milk. At about three weeks they start to take an interest in more solid food. The mother brings in the first food so if you feed a dry food diet make sure the biscuit is soaked so the kits can nibble at it. If feeding meat ensure that you remove any surplus. Flies are a great nuisance at this time of year and it does not take long for meat to get flyblown. The kits will now be growing at an alarming rate so you will need constant food for them.

Between the third and the fifth week their eyes will start to open which is the perfect time to start handling the kits. After plenty of handling and good food they will be weaned at six to eight weeks of age. When weaning, as with all animals, make it a slow process rather than risk emotional damage by just separating them all suddenly.

Ailments

The ferret is a bit of a hot potato where vets are concerned. Because they are closely related to the wild polecat, they tend to hide their health problems like their wild cousins do so by the time most owners realize that something is amiss it is too late for the vet to do anything about it. Another reason why ferrets are not always taken to the vet is that, because they are so cheap, people treat them like garden tools and when one is ill it is simply put down at home and a new one bought, just like a common or garden spade. This behaviour still goes on but, hopefully, as time goes by will become less frequent. At the end of the day it is up to the owner. Educate these people and who knows. Because the ferret is becoming more popular as a pet as well as a working animal vets are seeing more of them which is not only beneficial to the ferret but is also resulting in the charges of such treatments coming down all the while.

The following notes on ailments are just a guide to them, not a bible of first aid. These are the more common ailments you may encounter. The list of potential ailments is a staggering one but that is not what this book is about so I'll leave that to the vets.

If your ferret is ill, or you think something is wrong, take it to a qualified vet straight away, remembering how the ferret masks its illnesses. If you delay it might get past the point where the vet can help it. **So if in doubt - check it out.**

The next selection of ailments are the common ones you may encounter during routine health checks on your ferret. You will need to conduct regular checks to see if everything is okay and you should look at the following points:-

1. Feet

The feet of the ferret are the most important feature for without them the ferret cannot walk. This is why it is important that we look after them and ensure nothing untoward happens. Foot-rot was a common thing in years gone by but is less of a problem today. It is caused by dirty and damp conditions which enable a mite to develop which makes the feet swell and scab, and if not treated, the claws will drop off - ouch! If you encounter this, isolate the ferret at once, burn all the bedding and shavings, and thoroughly disinfect the hutch. Seek veterinary advice urgently.

The claws of a ferret are non-retractable and situated on each of the five toes on each foot. They can grow to an unmanageable level if not kept in check but that doesn't mean to say that you must cut them back all the time though. If the ferret is kept on a concrete floor the claws will be kept naturally short although they may still need clipping once as year. Ferrets on wooden floors will scratch the walls and floors to try to keep them down but again if the claw is too long and is inhibiting the free movement of the ferret they will need clipping.

The ferret's claw has a blood vessel inside it which must not be cut into. The claw can be clipped to a sensible, comfortable length for the animal using dogs' claw clippers. Cut the claws one by one to an equal length. If at any time you accidentally cut into the vein use a bar of soap or Vaseline to stem the flow. This is to be rubbed in whilst the ferret is kept still to overcome the initial shock.

2. Eyes

In the eventuality of there being a problem with a ferret's eyes, you should isolate the animal in a different cage (a hospital cage), just in case it is conjunctivitis. This is easily treated with a solution of Optrex, just the same as it is for humans. Wash the eye gently, using the solution, or a gauze with the solution on it. Remember to discard the gauze after use. Other eye problems can be caused by sawdust, scratches and foreign bodies. Again, care must be used while inspecting and cleaning the eye. When cleaning, clean from the inside corner (near the ear) to the side of the eye nearest the nose.

3. Skin/hair

As with most hairy animals, there are many things that need to be looked for. Fleas and ticks are the number one pest of the ferret owner. There are several other complaints I have come across including mange and baldness. These are dealt with in detail later on in this chapter.

4. Ears

Many ferret owners today clean their ferrets' ears to rid them of wax. This is often mistaken for the ear mite which causes an irritation, making the animal scratch uncontrollably. If left untreated the mite can enter the inner ear and this can lead to the death of the animal. The mite will cause a brown deposit with a slight smell. If you notice this quickly you can administer drops (cat drops) yourself, or play safe and visit the vet. The ferret will naturally have a certain amount of earwax which is needed to protect the inner ear and is usually hidden from view.

5. Teeth

All animals, especially carnivores, are prone to some sort of trouble with their teeth and the ferret is no different and should have regular checks of the teeth. When carrying out these checks you get your ferret used to having fingers in its mouth for which your vet will thank you one day. Some people even clean their ferrets' teeth with a smokers' toothpaste. A well handled ferret should pose no problem when having its teeth checked but if you come across a stubborn one a light pinch of the skin between the ears will suffice. What you feed your ferret can also affect its teeth. Some complete diets contain a certain amount of gravy which will stain the teeth. Although this does not harm the ferret some owners get worried when their prize and joy's teeth start turning brown for no apparent reason. Providing the ferret with a whole rabbit diet, or a carcass now and then, will help the teeth by cleaning them during eating, plus the calcium of the bones is good for the ferret's teeth.

Fleas

These are the one thing I can guarantee that your ferrets will get a visit from, however clean the housing. Fleas are contracted from other animals such as cats, dogs and, of course, rabbits. If fleas are encountered, all bedding and shavings must be destroyed, and the hutch/court disinfected. The ferrets can be treated with a number of products designed for cats and dogs.

NOTE: you will have to alter the dosage before treating your ferret. Ensure it is safe to use. Care must be taken if your ferret is pregnant or nursing young as there is a danger of poisoning.

Ticks

These are picked up in all sorts of places. Working ferrets usually pick them up around the head and neck regions. They lay dormant and wait for a host animal to feed on and once fed they will appear bloated from their host's blood. There are a number of good tick removers on the market today but forget all the old remedies - burning a tick off with a lighted cigarette is simply courting disaster. They can be treated with a flea spray or, alternatively, dabbed with surgical spirit or alcohol. After a while they will shrivel up and die. Do not let them drop off naturally as they will only complete their life cycle, resulting in more ticks.

Hair loss

Nothing is more alarming than finding that your ferret is going bald in places. This could be down to too many eggs in their diet, excessive molting, or simply old age. Pregnant jills sometimes appear tatty and moth-eaten but this disappears later.

Mange is another cause. Mange is caused by an *ectoparasite* attacking the skin. This then lays its eggs under the skin, causing irritation, scratching and loss of hair. Foxes are the most common carriers but any animal can catch it. In humans it is called scabies. Seek veterinary help if you suspect your animal has mange.

Abscesses

These are simply a wound that has filled with pus. These can be caused by bites, infected stings or a foreign body puncturing the skin. An abscess may respond to a course of antibiotics or it may need lancing, sometimes both.

Heatstroke

The ferret wasn't designed for heat so it cannot handle high temperatures. Would you with a fur coat like theirs? Because they cannot sweat the only way for a ferret to cool itself is by panting - just like a dog. Funnily enough, this used to be called the sweats. Ferrets should never be put in a situation in which they are likely to suffer from this. Think carefully about the position of the hutch and never leave the ferrets' box in a hot car. If you are showing your ferrets it is a good idea to take a water bottle with a mister (just like you use for plants), to cool down the ferrets in warm weather.

Use your common sense!

Aleutian disease

This was first discovered on the Aleutian strain of mink, hence the name. The disease is a *parvovirus* and attacks the immune system. The disease can spread to all ferrets, parents to young, stranger to stranger. It is spread by the fluids of ferrets, the urine and droppings, blood and saliva which is why it is important to take care in the breeding season and in the removal of jills from *oestrus.*

Just as with the common cold, it can be broadcast via the low volume mist emitted from the ferret's mouth by breathing, coughing or the dreaded sneeze. These mists can travel an incredible distance.

The symptoms of this disease vary. Aggressiveness, fever, paralysis, loss of weight and dark tarry droppings are all signs that something is amiss, with death not far away. Unfortunately there is no specific treatment for this disease but steroids and antibiotics will give temporary relief.

Diagnosis can be obtained by the usual method of a blood sample which can be obtained from a clipped toe. In the eventuality of a ferret dying suddenly, a post mortem should always be carried out. This will not only detect any disease but also find out if it is contagious. When you have lost one animal you don't want to risk the others. If you have any ferrets that suffer from Aleutian, they must under no circumstances be bred from.

These are just a few of the more common ailments but remember:

IF IN DOUBT - CHECK IT OUT

Chapter 6

Know your quarry- the rabbit

The rabbit is a major agricultural pest, but it wasn't always that way. The rabbit was introduced to these shores by the Normans, not only as a valuable source of food but for their fur as well. Rabbit meat was, and still is, a meal that can offer a higher percentage of protein with less fat than pork, chicken, lamb or beef. Add to this the potential use of the fur for protection and this made the humble rabbit a valuable commodity.

The rabbit spread and can now be found all over Britain and Ireland. It was not long before people caught on and many landowners and estates developed and kept huge warrens of rabbits, purely for food and clothing. The people who looked after the rabbits were called 'warreners,' a name that will stick with the rabbiter for life. The rabbit numbers kept rising and rising until in the 1800s they became a pest to the ever growing agricultural scene. More and more damage was being reported so the government had to do something. Various laws were brought in to combat the rising numbers. As previously rabbiting was confined to the noble few, punishment for poaching was severe (does Australia ring a bell?) but a new law, the Ground Game Act made it possible for any tenant to hunt the rabbit. By the turn of the twentieth century up to 100 million rabbits were caught annually.

The government were so concerned that they drafted in extra laws to designate the whole of England and Wales a rabbit clearance area, giving all landowners the obligation to control rabbits on their own land.

During 1950 rabbit damage cost a staggering £50,000,000 but as the government were discussing how to control the numbers a disease was hitting our shores in the south that would change the nation's perception of the rabbit forever.

Myxomatosis is a disease that was developed on the Continent to control the millions of rabbits. The disease is carried by the rabbit flea, so spreading from wild to domestic rabbits is not a problem. This flea was thought to have been carried by birds coming over from France and it found a native rabbit and the disease soon spread. The ears, eyes and bottom of a diseased rabbit swell, emitting a bright pus.

During 1953-54 the numbers dwindled down to just 1% of the previous year. Yes, 99% of all rabbits had perished from a slow and painful death. The saviours, funnily enough, were the runts and outcasts of the warrens. These rabbits were forced to live outside the warren, above ground, and away from the rabbit flea infested burrows.

Slowly the rabbit hit back, the strains of myxy getting weaker by the year. By the 1970s the rabbit population was becoming immune to myxy.

Today there is a new disease which is threatening to wipe out the rabbit once more, Viral Hemorrhagic Disease. V.H.D. has been recorded in the U.K. in the 1990s. This disease takes 1- 2 days from start to finish with the animal dying in a fit condition, unlike myxy. It has been feared that this can spread like myxy but up until now there have only been local, sporadic outbreaks. Rabbits in the U.K. seem to have some immunity to the disease and today it has been estimated that rabbit damage annually is over £150 million a year, with the potential to double.

Because rabbit numbers were rising, interest in the control of them rose again. Ferrets and lurchers became popular once more. When we need to control an animal, we must first understand how it lives and where we can find it.

The male rabbit is known as a **buck** and the female a **doe**. The male can weigh between one and two kilos and in turn can eat up to 25% of its body weight of green vegetable matter per day. As with all animals the female is smaller and more petite than the male.

These animals usually breed from January until August but with more and more mild winters we are experiencing births all year round. The early born can reproduce at four months old. Having a gestation period of 28-30 days it has been calculated that in perfect conditions a doe having five litters a year each containing five youngsters could be responsible for more than *4,000* rabbits in three years. I know the chance of this happening is slim but it just shows why the rabbit has a reputation for being a sexually orientated animal.

The young are not born in the main warren but in a **stop**. This is a tunnel of about three feet long and the young are inside with the end sealed. Mother comes once daily to suckle the young until weaned at 21-28 days old.

Over 90% of rabbits die before their first year is over, most of them within the first three months so when you are surveying an area, if you see a lot of really young rabbits there is a good chance that it is not the main warren, just a nursery. Rabbits live in a system of tunnels called burrows which when connected are a warren. The warren may contain anything from 2 to 200 entrances and this is the area for the ferret to do its work.

Rabbits move from this safe haven to search for food. The more rabbits in a colony the greater the amount of food that will be consumed in the area. A rabbit may have to travel a field or two for good nutritious food and they can re-colonise at an alarming rate.

Before you embark on your day's ferreting you will need to do a survey, to see where the areas of damage are, where the warrens are, and also the safe and not so safe working areas. The rabbit can inflict a large amount of damage. There are not many crops or cereals that these little creatures haven't a taste for. It has been calculated that on a field of winter wheat the rabbit can inflict a 1% yield loss per hectare. That is a staggering 65 kg of wheat per rabbit based on the number of ears lost and the loss of grain per ear.

Take a look around and look for the tell tale signs:-

1. Rabbit scrapes, runs and droppings.

2. Damage to crops, buildings and forestry.

Look at night with a powerful lamp and ask locals for their knowledge of the land. You can then make up your mind where to ferret first, and by which method.

Chapter 7

Finding your quarry

To successfully carry out ferreting you must first find the home of the rabbit, the warren. This can be situated in all sorts of positions, usually (but not always) in the least accessible part of the field. Just because a field has a lot of rabbits feeding in it does not necessarily mean that they live there - rabbits frequently cover a field or two in search for quality food.

Having carried out your surveillance you will hopefully have spotted the following:-

1. Crop damage

2. Droppings

3. Rabbits in the field

4. Scrape

*5. Entrances or bolt
holes from the warren*

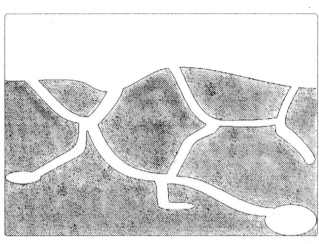

All of the above signal the presence of rabbit, but it is the warren that we are interested in. These can vary from a simple two holer to a complex and ancient warren with a couple of hundred holes.

Before you use your ferrets on new land this sort of surveillance is a necessity. Ignore this advice and you will follow the fate of many a ferreter who thought he knew best. In ferreting, experience will teach you a lot when you are preparing to use your animals. Get all the help and information you can and in time you will be able to decide what suits you best.

As you can see from these photographs, it doesn't take many rabbits to damage the land. There may be as many as 2 - 5 times the amount of rabbits actually living and feeding on the land as seen there.

Rabbits cause all sorts of damage, from livestock to crops, so it is vital that the warren complex is understood properly. As you can see the warren is made up from a series of tunnels, both free flowing and ones with stops in. Mounds of earth excavated from the warren usually signal the main entrances to the warren.

This is the place for your ferrets to work. To understand how the rabbit lives will help you overcome the problems they can cause you on a day's ferreting.

Chapter 8

Ferreting equipment

Ferrets can be worked in a number of ways, most of which can be combined. You can work with nets, shoot over the ferrets, or with a dog or a hawk. There are numerous combinations so I will keep it simple.

First, let's look at the equipment that you will need for any ferreting trip. The most vital is the permission to do so, without which you won't be going hunting. To begin with it can be very difficult to gain permission but be determined and prepared to take the lows with the highs.

Your first port of call should be to the local ferreters. During my time promoting ferreting at shows, I get overwhelmed by the number of young, would-be ferreters who just cannot get a break. I believe education is the way to save our sport but how can we teach people when they are not allowed to learn? Landowners are suspicious of novice ferreters as they have been caught out before with promises of good timekeeping and reliability which all go down the pan when the weather turns. Once bitten, twice shy, so show them that you are reliable.

Become a member of the Countryside Alliance or B.A.S.C. and ask their regional office for local contacts. I mention joining these organisations as everybody who participates in any country sport, ferreting or otherwise, should be a member. Not only do they offer excellent insurance packages, they are essential when seeking permission.

We live in an age when many people misunderstand our way of life and are constantly trying to ban it. We have freedom of choice, a choice to participate in legal sports, and we intend to keep it that way.

Trying to gain permission today is a lot different from, say, ten to twenty years ago. Many farmers have had their vision of the ferret blighted by not so thoughtful people in the past. Be vigilant; target the local farmers and gamekeepers or local shooting clubs. Wildfowling or shooting clubs have many different sorts of members, usually one or two ferreters. When you do have an appointment, beware; first impressions count.

Wear smart, respectable clothes, clean your car, don't go in your work or ferreting clothes so that you don't look like the local tramp. Point out the benefits you can provide and perhaps, in the case of keepers, offer your services for beating. Indicate the areas of rabbit damage and explain how you can help. Once you have gained permission word often spreads like wildfire.

This is how I started many moons ago, helping a local dairy farmer. When that farm disbanded I searched for another place to ferret. I was persistent to the point of annoyance but as the ferrets worked, the word spread. I now have more permission than I can use sensibly and I try to pass it on to other ferreters.

Your reputation is at risk if you give permission and you should only do so with the landowner or farmer's agreement. In that way the farmer is not under the illusion that it is you who is controlling the rabbits or you could find yourself in the same position as the following ferreter.

Because a large amount of land needed controlling the permission was to be shared. Both had areas to control so there was no need to cross onto each other's patch. Imagine the horror of the original ferreter to be told at the local clay shoot of someone rabbiting on the patch he was about to do. On investigation he found large deep holes left unfilled, nets set on holes near a footpath - a nightmare scenario.

It took many phone calls and meetings not only to convince the landowner that it wasn't the original ferreter but also to keep the permission itself so be warned. Sadly, this is a common tale which is why it is so hard to get permission in the first place. It is your duty to convince and promise that you will do everything in your power to leave the land in the state in which you found it.

For the beginner the basic requirements for ferreting will be few but will grow with time. Ferreting has a magical quality about it; it is a sport that can be as cheap or as expensive as you make it.

Once you have either gained permission or found a ferreter to share permission with, you will need ferrets. That's the object of this book. One of the beauties of ferreting is the mysterious nature of the rabbit. No two warrens are alike. So how many ferrets will you need?

The ferret puts in an immense amount of work during a day's hunt, a fact that is often overlooked. A tired ferret tends to struggle and more than often ends up in a 'lie up' which results in unwanted digging. Ensure that you have enough ferrets for the amount of work planned for the day. Work a bury and rest a bury. For the majority of trips four ferrets are ample, and just two for the smaller ones. The size of the warren, and amount of warren, worked in a day has a major bearing on the number of ferrets needed. A warrener I know on the local estate can use up to fifty ferrets during the day, sometimes working them all at once in the many areas on the estate. He mainly uses albinos. To avoid confusion they are split into groups, which live together and are marked with an animal friendly livestock marker, just like the ones used on sheep and pigs.

The colour of the ferret (as discussed earlier) makes no difference physically, but mentally colour can play a big role. The colours can make a big difference whilst working. Some prefer the white of the albino, some the dark polecat and all the varied colours in-between.

The albino, because it is white, stands out well in thick, dense undergrowth and grassland, but not in deep frost or a layer of snow. Some areas of Great Britain get more of the white stuff than others and they prefer the dark colours. Remember, the only difference is just a different hair colour.

The age at which the ferret is worked varies dramatically. I tend to compare the entering of ferrets to that of entering a dog. You must make sure that the animal is mature enough, trained enough, and started slowly. If the ferrets are the young of the summer, wait until the turn of January. The ferrets will then be about seven or eight months old. Used to being handled in all situations they should be ready to start, but there are always exceptions. They might take a little longer but remember, you have several years of work ahead of you... an extra month or two isn't going to hurt, is it?

Start them in a simple warren, a nice four-holer with a gradually sloping entrance hole, preferably behind an experienced ferret. Don't try to force the ferret down a steep hole or any other, just let nature take its course. If you force a ferret down or go to snatch it from the hole you might encourage it to skulk. This is when the ferret comes to the surface of the hole but keeps just out of hands' reach. This can be overcome with time and encouragement, but prevention is better than cure.

You will need something to transport your ferrets in, the main requirements being practicality and security. When the ferret is seen or mentioned the first image is that of sticking them down one's trousers. You may laugh but this was one of many madcap methods of transporting ferrets about. When ferreting was confined to the noble few, poachers had to carry their animals around without them being noticed. A small pocket was sewn into the trouser waist and the ferret was placed inside. After all, they weren't going to walk around with it in a hardy box for all to see, were they? This method was for the brave; let's stick with more conventional means. But what is conventional?

The earliest ferreters used sacks for transportation but what about the poor ferret? Sacks were not only cold but offered the ferret no comfort and no protection either. A better way had to be found. Boxes of all shapes and sizes were used; wicker, wood, metal and lately, plastic. Because of the nature of the ferret, security was the main concern as these animals are the Houdinis of the animal world. Some of these materials weren't ideally suited to the needs of the ferret as in the case of the metal boxes. Metal heats up in the summer causing the inside to sweat but more alarming is the impact in winter. The metal freezes in the winter months causing all sorts of unthinkable injuries to the ferrets' skin. So a more manageable source began to be used - wood.

This is a better material and gives the opportunity for all sorts of different designs. Many boxes have been tried and tested and the more practical ones copied throughout the country.

There are many different designs of boxes. The ideal size of a box is 8 ins. x 18 ins. (200mm. x 450mm.) with a wide comfortable strap. This ensures that the box can be carried safely for both ferrets and ferreter. Wire cages and cat carriers can be, and indeed are, used in warm weather for travelling.

Electronic Ferret Finders

One of the many improvements in the world of the ferret, especially the working ferret, has been the ferret detector. Before this modern technology was designed, there were several ways of ferret retrieval. The majority of ferrets were coped (muzzled), or had their teeth broken or sawn off, to prevent them from killing - all acts of gross cruelty to the ferret.

In the early days ferreters worked the jills loose but kept the hob confined which made him lonely and resentful. When a jill below ground layed up the hob was released to find the jill and her quarry. He would be wearing a collar to which was attached a rope 25 yards long with knots at one yard intervals. Because of his solitary way of life he was a jealous creature and he thought that he should have whatever the jill had so he would drive her off. The jill would surface and be boxed up and the ferreter would then follow the line and dig out the hob and the rabbit. Just imagine what these ferreters had to go through. Picture the scene. Perhaps ten yards of line had been used but the ferret might have gone four yards forward, one sideward and four back. You could think that the ferret is 30 feet from you when it was actually only a couple away. Just imagine how many digs were required to find the ferret. Many still advocate this method, some even swear by it, I suppose it's the age we live in. But why dig three or four holes instead of just one?

Because of substances encountered underground it is advisable to cover the transmitter on the collar with electricians' waterproof tape which will not only keep it safe and dry but will

The locater comes in two depths, eight and fifteen feet. The transmitter is carried on a leather collar which fits around the ferret's neck.

prevent the screw top from working loose. It is also handy to put a brightly coloured tape around the receiver. If only I had a pound for the times one has been put down and temporarily lost because of its drab grey colouring. When the ferret is underground and the ferreter wants to find it, the receiver box is switched on. The switch is put to the maximum depth to start with.

With a sweeping movement cover the ground under which the ferret is working. Carry on until the box beeps like a Geiger counter which means that the ferret has been found. Slowly reduce the depth until the area you are sweeping has reduced to a square foot. The centre of this foot is the sweet spot. The depth is at the minimum that the receiver will pick up. This is the spot in which to start digging.

When the ferret is working there are several reasons why it may refuse to return to the surface. It may have forced a rabbit into a 'stop' and is refusing to leave its prey, it could have killed a rabbit below ground or, as I will explain, the ferret could be trapped in one of the many passages inside the warren.

While ferreting can bring many problems, 'trapping' can be a potentially lethal one. This is where the transmitter comes into its own. The warren was designed for rabbits which are considerably larger than ferrets, therefore the width of the burrows are as large as the rabbit. The ferret can sometimes find this to be a difficulty when working. One of the features of the warren is a 'stop' and these can point in all directions. These are the rabbits' safe spots. Because rabbits have very few nerves in their rear quarters, they feel no pain there and use them as a defence mechanism when threatened. The rabbit squeezes into the stop, head first, with its rear protecting it. When these passages are vertical or drop down to another stop the rabbit uses its body to grip the sides thus enabling it to negotiate a sheer drop or climb. But unfortunately, as the ferret is smaller it cannot copy this move by the rabbit. The ferret is now trapped, unable to climb. With the invention of the locater this is a problem easily overcome.

When digging to your ferret care should be taken. The spade of an over-active digger often injures ferrets. Not only is there the danger of decapitation but of loose soil falling in and suffocating the animal.

The probe is used to check the depth of the void of the burrow from the surface where you are digging. This tool is invaluable when dealing with these vertical drops. When you begin to dig remember to start the hole at the centre of the reading and work outwards from this reading. If turf has to be removed place upside down, and put all of the removed earth on top of it. Because some ferrets move when the thuds of the spade are heard, every now and then check the locater to make sure where it is.

When you have reached to within a foot of your reading test the direction with the probe. This will enable you to break through to the exact spot of the burrow. When you have broken through, be extra careful not to let the hole cave in. As with a lot of things in ferreting, experience is the best source of knowledge. After a few digs you will know what to do and perfect your digging skills.

Dogs

Many a countryman has a dog as a companion, the same goes for the ferreter. Many different types can be used; lurchers, terriers, or gundogs if the rabbits are to be shot. As with shooting, there is no place for an unruly or disobedient dog in the field. Dogs can be used to mark the occupied warrens, catch fleeing rabbits or retrieve wounded game. There are many books on the market concerned with the training of the ferreter's dog and as this book is about ferrets I would suggest these other books for advice on training dogs.

Knives

No country man or woman should ever leave home without a knife. With the rise in popularity of multi-functional knives, more people are using these today but many still use the traditional lock or sheaf knife. Whatever knife you use make sure it is sharp. A blunt knife is only good for stirring your tea!

Probe

This is a long metal 'T' bar used for probing the soil to find the exact position of the burrow. Some have a bulge about four inches from the tip which will move freely when the probe has broken through to the burrow.

Trap-box

This is a box that has been designed around a conventional cage trap, but with solid sides. This I have seen used to marvellous effect by the warreners on the Raveningham estate in Norfolk.

Nets

There are two types of net commonly used; the purse net and the long net.

The **purse net** is made from either hemp or the modern fabric, nylon. Hemp nets were the traditional netting used, as opposed to the newer nylon but there are drawbacks. Comparisons show that the two could not be further apart. While the hemp is an easily handled but expensive, heavy, absorbent material which needs constant treatment after use the modern nylon is a cheaper, light netting that dries very quickly but it is not as easy to handle. This is often overlooked and compensated for by the availability of these nets. You can buy them almost anywhere.

The other net used by the rabbiter is the **long net**. Although long netting is a sport itself these nets can be, and are, used in conjunction with purse nets, aiding both dog and gun. Using these as stop nets has the problem that the rabbit sometimes will dart from hole to hole, not bolting cleanly. Although a lot of people will want to ignore this fact, it happens. That is why the vast majority of rabbits shot are going from hole to hole. Of course a lot depends on the location but you have been warned. If you are interested in long-netting, there are some interesting contacts at the rear of this book.

Spade

Sometimes called a graft, the spade plays a bigger part in ferreting than most people realize. As it is the tool that will be used to retrieve your ferrets, you will have to make sure it is the right one. Tradition alone does not dig the hole for you. In the small areas of Suffolk and Norfolk in which I ferret you would be amazed at the different soil structures I encounter. Sandy dunes, fine soil by the coast, through to the clays of the East Anglian farms. That it is why the choice of spade or spades is vital. Hard wearing, sharp edged, but more importantly comfortable to the user, the spade must be able to dig efficiently into whatever soil is present, including the depth. Remember that could be up to and beyond 8 feet in depth.

Pictures and stories of people using long handled grafts are ideal, if they are practicable. Because of the varied soils I use an angled head and handle spade. This enables all soils at any depth to be dug out successfully.

Odds and Sods

I have outlined the essential tools for a day's ferreting but these are some non-essentials that are always wanted when you don't have them. Some of these items might seem a bit ridiculous but let me assure you, they work.

An assortment of ground clearance tools ranging from a scythe or billhook to secateurs are handy when you have to do some drastic clearance.

Constant kneeling in wet and cold conditions can play havoc with your knees. Gardeners' knee pads can not only save you grief now but in many years to come and the same could be said for gloves as well.

Encountering clay and ballast whilst digging is a frustrating experience, but what can you use to speed up the retrieval of both ferret and hopefully rabbit? Across the country you can find army surplus stores which are Aladdin's caves for many a sportsperson. After several struggles with compacted clay, I used a mini pick-axe/shovel and this is always kept in the car now having saved the day many times.

One item that should be carried by all, but sadly isn't, is a first-aid kit. Probably the most under-rated piece of equipment, it is often forgotten. Because of the nature of ferreting, the wild, often remote locations, and the equipment used, a first aid kit is often needed, not only by your animals but for you and your friends as well.

Clothing

Clothing for the ferreter plays a major part in the health and well being of, yes, the ferreter. Firstly it keeps you warm, dry, and hopefully, prevents you from sticking out like a beacon. By this I mean not to wear brightly coloured garments, however warm they may be.

Although the rabbit is colour blind, in its world of greys a bright colour will show up. This will not only alarm it into bolting but any rabbits sitting rough will head in the opposite direction. Greens blend into the surroundings and also do not attract unwanted attention to you.

Because of the time of year that you will be spending at the beck and call of nature there are two vital areas of your body to keep warm and dry - your head and feet, of course. Keep these happy and the rest of your body will feel the benefit.

During the time that you spend walking, digging and standing about, if you wear inadequate footwear your feet will suffer. Make sure your choice is the right one, after all, they're your feet. Be it a good stout pair of boots or wellingtons, make sure they are man enough for the job ahead.

Hats vary, some simple, some extreme but again, make sure they will do the job. Spectacle wearers have an extra problem with rain so a peaked cap or bushman's is the order of the day. From woolly hats to the bushman's all have their ups and downs. Get what suits the job, whatever it may look like to an outsider.

As rabbiting is mainly carried out in the harsher time of year, a good jacket is required. A good quality wax jacket is possibly the most versatile, although waxes tend to be cold, unlike quilt-ed or tweed fabrics but remember, it will be wet, dirty and thorny. What jacket suits these conditions? The waxed one. Waxed over-trousers should also be a part of the kit. Chaps are used by some but these have no protection for your bottom so remember this before sitting down on the grass

Chapter 9

The ferret at work

Assuming you have your ferrets, equipment and permission, how do these creatures work? The basics of the working ferret are the same for whatever form of ferreting you have decided to participate in. Whether the ferret is being shot over, has a dog or hawk waiting for the bolting rabbits or the warren is being netted, the ferret works in the same way below ground.

The whole aim of ferreting is for the ferret to evict (bolt) the rabbit from its warren so it can be caught by one the methods stated earlier. The rabbit is classed as a pest species, but one with a difference. The classic example of why an animal is classed as a pest is being in the wrong place at the wrong time. Put the rabbit in a nice hutch at the bottom of the garden and it is a popular pet. This is the fact that the vast majority of the public finds hard to come to terms with. That is why it is important that ferreting is carried out humanely, efficiently and safely at all times.

Surveillance is essential in ensuring the day runs smoothly. Having taken a look at the ground that is about to be worked a number of questions are raised. If nets are to be used, will I need to trim the entrances of the warren in advance? Ensure enough nets are taken. Will I need extra help ferreting?

If you are using a hawk or a dog this will be not be important, but if you are shooting you will have to think about the safety of both the ferrets and the people who are shooting. Guns present must be 101% safe and aware of the difference between a ferret and a rabbit. Come to think of it, if they can't tell the difference, they shouldn't be there in the first place. There is no place for an unsafe gun in any day's shooting, not just ferreting.

Check your equipment as there is nothing worse than getting ready to ferret, or indeed to get halfway through the day, and realise that a vital piece of equipment has either been left at home or doesn't work. Ferret collars and receivers must be checked and it is a good idea to have some spare batteries near.

On the morning of the day's ferreting, box up the ferrets that are going to be used and make sure that they are not hungry. Don't let them gorge themselves though otherwise they will only want to sleep. These ferrets will need all their energy, there's a lot of work to be done today.

Imagine the day is planned, ferreting partners informed and the ferrets ready. The day's ferreting will be using both nets and guns. Having packed the essential flask, biscuits, ferrets and equipment we set off for the day's sport. The area to be controlled today is a field containing some steep ditches and shrubs.

Upon arrival we take a walk round with the gun and dogs, not only to see if there are any rabbits sitting rough but to send the remainder below ground (to ferret them out they first need to be below ground). We will be using the nets first in the ditch. When we use the nets on a day like this it is always useful to have a gun stand overlooking the area just in case of an undiscovered bolt hole. This is just my preference, others use lurchers, some just look and curse themselves for missing that dreaded bolt-hole.

Before the ferrets can be entered all the holes must be netted. The nets are set over the holes by pulling the rings apart on the unravelled net. To set the net place the bottom ring (opposite to the ring nearest the peg) inside the hole, place the net over the hole and peg it down securely. The aim is for the rabbit to run over the bottom ring and into the net which then purses and the rabbit is caught.

The most common mistakes made by novices when setting nets are to overlook the bolt holes, not securing the nets strongly enough with the pegs and letting the nets become full of twigs and debris whilst setting them but this will pass with experience. Sometimes Mother Nature's obstacles hinder the setting of the net; tree trunks, large entrance holes and hard ground. All will test the patience but persevere and it will be worthwhile.

The nets are set, standing gun is ready; now all we need are the ferrets. Because the warren is about a dozen holes we are using a couple of ferrets with the scope to add another couple if necessary. On go the collars and these are tested with the receiver, just to make sure all is working. These collars have revolutionized ferreting but are a major pain when using nets. The collar, because of its transmitter protruding, makes it hard for the ferret to pass through the net without disturbing it. Some ferrets acquire this knack but the bigger hobs find it hard though not impossible. When entering the ferret, find a nice entrance hole that slopes slightly, not one with a steep drop.

The ferrets are now working and hopefully a rabbit will appear soon, but you will have to be careful. Rats, stoats, little owls, cats, foxes and birds can all be underground so there is a chance of something unusual being bolted into or through your purse net. The beauty of purse nets is that if any animals were to be bolted you could set them free and no damage would be done. Bear this in mind if your ferrets flatly refuse to enter a burrow; the ferret knows best. If it is the ferrets' first season, they will be a little bit excited, tails fluffed out like bottle cleaners but all that hard work you put in by handling and socializing them when they were kits will pay off. It just takes time.

Several minutes have passed, no ferrets and no rabbits. The ferret has surfaced for a second and then continued working. When a ferret surfaces it is usually a sign that there is something down there but refusing to play ball and bolt. If there was nothing down there the ferret would surface continually with little enthusiasm to go back down so this is a good sign.

As the receiver box is about to be deployed the silence is broken. After several unmistakable thumps heard from under our feet, a rabbit bursts out of a hole. Is it netted or did we miss one and it will escape through a bolthole? It was netted. The rabbit is lying motionless, enclosed in a perfectly pursed net. Now this animal has to be dispatched, and quickly. There are two methods of despatching the rabbit, both of which need to be taught by an experienced hand if you are a newcomer to the sport. The 'chop' method (shown below, left) is as the name implies. A sharp blow to the neck by either a priest or your hands will kill the rabbit immediately. The other method (below, right) is a bit harder but more effective. Take hold of the rabbit, either by the midriff or legs, place your thumb behind the rabbit's neck, stretch its body and at the same time push the head backwards. This will break the neck and death is instant and humane.

This can be carried out in the net or otherwise, whatever you feel most comfortable with. When the rabbit is removed don't just chuck it in a pile, empty the bladder. This is done by hold-

ing the rabbit up by its shoulders and feeling down the stomach towards the rear end. This will then empty the bladder. Place them in a row ready for transporting or you could 'leg' them. Get hold of one of the rear legs and cut a slot behind the tendon, then place the other leg through this slot. The rabbit can then be carried on a stick. This is invaluable when a big bag is achieved.

After a flurry of rabbits bolting, one of which is shot because of an overlooked bolthole, the ferrets start to surface and they are picked up and boxed. If a ferret refuses to leave the entrance of a hole, playing the fool at the entrance, this is called 'skulking.' Although not unusual for the novice ferret, it is an annoying habit that must be broken. Usually you can coax out the ferret with a dead rabbit or a drink of milk from the car, if it is handy. This should do the trick. Do not let frustration beat you and attempt to drag the ferret out - this will only make matters worse.

All but one of the ferrets have been accounted for. After a quick search with the receiver box the rogue animal was found, three feet down. The ferret has 'laid up.' This is either because the ferret has killed below ground and stayed with the rabbit, is stuck behind the rabbit or, as is common, the rabbit has reached one of its stops. This is a tunnel with a dead end. The rabbit will squeeze into this and stick its rear end out at the ferret but the ferret doing what comes naturally to it will try to kill it. (Ferreting can be full of contradictions, For example, we want the ferret to bolt the rabbit but the ferret wants to obey its instincts and kill it). The ferret will then stay with the rabbit. A dig will be needed, out comes the spade.

When digging you must remember that what comes out you will have to return. Nothing does more damage to any country sport than the sight of ignorance. In the past, too many ferreters have been refused permission through these actions. Start digging in the centre of the located spot. Keep the receiver box on just in case the ferret moves. When you are about a foot away get the probe and feel for the burrow. This tool makes the finding much quicker and safer for the ferret. Before you have broken through bear in mind the whereabouts of the ferret. It can be easy to break through and decapitate the ferret below. Once you have broken through, you should be on top of the ferret; pick it up and retrieve the rabbit. After this check the void for an other. It has been known for up to six rabbits to be in one dead end, the most I have encountered is four my most being four. Now that both rabbit and ferret are retrieved the hole can be filled in.

Now the nets need to be picked up, folded and put back in the bag. The rest of the holes will be ferreted with a team of guns. When shooting bolting rabbits safety must come first, for both the ferret and the people around the guns. If the people shooting aren't used to the surroundings nothing will be more tempting than the bolting rabbit. When shooting rabbits with ferrets you can cover almost any type of terrain, be it open ground or thick hedgerows and woodland. The standing guns must be placed at strategic points so they can shoot the rabbits safely without risking ferret or human life. This is sometimes tested when shooting either side of a thick hedge, which is why it is vital that everyone is 101% safe and will listen to the person in charge of the ferrets.

The actual working of ferrets is the same as described earlier but without the nets. When shooting though, you tend to see less clean bolts into the open and more hole to hole bolts. Accidents do happen, but 99% of them can be avoided. It is no good afterwards saying that you thought the polecat ferret was a rabbit in the undergrowth. You must be certain, otherwise you shouldn't be there in the first place.

When working your ferrets there might be a time when luck runs out and one of your ferrets is missing. Many methods can be used; blocking all but one hole, digging a pit for the ferret to fall in and become trapped, placing the carrying box at the open hole. The method I suggest, although (touch wood) I have never had to use it, is the box-trap method. One of the warreners at Raveningham in Norfolk, Jim, devised a box similar to a cage trap but with solid sides and a caged window on top. This is devised so that when the ferret enters it stands on the step and the door shuts. The ferret will readily enter because it is dark inside. It is caught by its curiosity. This device is used a lot on the estate due to the ferrets being worked in groups of anything up to fifty. The ferrets are always caught up.

The difference in the methods of working ferrets varies enormously, from a pair of ferrets right up to fifty, Whether all with collars or all loose, and either a liner or a collared liner, depends on the scale of land, rabbits and time allocated to ferreting. This is the beauty of ferreting - experience will tell you which method suits you best.

When you have finished and are back at home think of the animals that have provided the day's sport first, the ferrets. Check for any injuries before returning them to their homes. Check the ferret finders, remove batteries and clean both transmitter and receiver. All the nets should be hung to dry, checking for any damage as you do this. This will ensure that when you get ready for your next outing there will be no surprises.

At the end of the day the ferrets' welfare is the most important factor. Look after your ferrets and they will provide you with outstanding sport and companionship for years to come.

Chapter 10

Ferreting and the law

When working your ferrets there are a number of legal requirements that may help or hinder you. These will not only affect
how your animals are kept but also how you treat the ferrets'
quarry.

These laws are there for everyone to see, but not enough actually learn them. This is a pity as they are useful if either anyone
approaches you whilst ferreting or you want to finally convince
that neighbouring farmer to let you control the rabbits.

You will get not just respect but probably more permission if
you show a professional attitude whilst going about your business. Remember, every time you go out it is the whole of country sports you are representing, not just yourself!

Pest Act 1954

Rabbit Clearance Orders (Under Section 1)

Rabbit Clearance Order No. 148, issued in 1972, made the
whole of England and Wales a rabbit clearance area (excluding
the City of London, the Isles of Scilly and Skokholm Island).

Occupiers' Responsibilities in Rabbit Clearance Area (Under
Section 1)

All occupiers have a continuing obligation to control rabbits living on, or resorting to, their land unless they can establish that
it is not reasonably practicable for them to do so, when they
must prevent the rabbits from doing damage, e.g. by fencing
them in with rabbit-proof fencing. Failure to fulfil his obligation may lead to the occupier being prosecuted or the work
being carried out at his expense.

Spread of Myxomatosis (Under Section 12)

It is illegal to use an infected rabbit to spread myxomatosis.

The Wild Mammals (Protection) Act 1996

This Act plugs a loophole that existed in wildlife legislation, where non-captive wild animals had little or no protection. It made it an offence to: 'mutilate, kick, beat, impale, stab, burn, stone, crush, drown, drag or asphyxiate any wild animal with intent to inflict unnecessary suffering.'

Exceptions allow pest control, shooting, hunting and coursing to be carried out providing that the animal is killed swiftly. This eliminates drowning as a means of dispatching trapped animals.

Agriculture Act 1947

Under Section 98 any person having the right to do so may, by written notice, be required by the Minister to take such steps as may be necessary for the killing, taking or destruction of certain animals or birds (or their eggs) for the purpose of preventing damage to crops, pasture, animal or human foodstuffs, livestock, trees, hedges, banks or any works on land. The notice may specify time limits for any action, the steps to be taken and the land on which they are to be taken.

Animals that may be specified in the notice are rabbits, hares, other rodents, deer, foxes and moles. There are powers to add other animals to the list. The birds that may be specified are all wild birds not protected by Schedule 1 of the Wildlife and Countryside Act 1981. Under Section 98 (7) (added by Section 2 of the Pests Act 1954) an occupier may be required by written notice to destroy or reduce breeding places or cover (e.g. scrub) for rabbits or to prevent rabbits from spreading or doing damage elsewhere.

Under Section 99 occupiers of land may be required to take

steps to prevent the escape of animals from land on which they are kept in captivity, but only if the animals are agricultural pests or animals which might damage banks or landworks. Dangerous animals are not included - they are the responsibility of local authorities.

Useful contacts:

Countryside Alliance
367 Kennington Road
London
SE11 4PT
Tel: 020 7582 5432
Fax: 020 7793 8484
PR Fax:0020 7793 8899

Brian + Carol Brinded
Quality rabbit longnets, purse nets and accessories.
Stable Cottage, Mill Road, East Bergholt, Suffolk, CO7 6UP
Tel: 01206 299281 Mobile/Answerphone 0468 008863

Ferreting Association for the control of rabbits.
Kim Lathaen Tel: 01341 423057
Tom Sturgess Tel: 023 8087 3381

National Ferret Welfare Society
113 Henry Street, Kenilworth, Leamington Spa, CU8 2HL

Wessex Ferret Club
c/o Robin Tarrant, P.O. Box 372, Southampton, Hampshire,
SO14 02A